Do's and Don'ts for Family Members

How to Pull Your Life Together When You're Suffering

About the pamphlet
When we're living with a chemically dependent person, most of us get caught up in trying to change that person—to the point of not taking care of ourselves. In this pamphlet the author guides us gently back to focusing on ourselves. Through reading these wise words, and working the exercises, we can begin to learn how to live a sane, productive life.

About the author
Terence Williams, M.A., is a writer and family therapist. He is the author of the book *I Won't Wait Up Tonight,* published by Hazelden. Williams was a manager of Family Services at Hazelden Foundation until 1991. His M.A. is from the University of Kansas, and he also did postgraduate work at Georgetown University in family systems theory and family psychotherapy.

Hazelden Classics for Families

Do's and Don'ts for Family Members
How to Pull Your Life Together When You're Suffering

Revised Edition

Terence Williams, M.A.

HAZELDEN®

Hazelden
Center City, Minnesota 55012-0176

1-800-328-9000
1-651-213-4590 (Fax)
www.hazelden.org

ISBN-13: 978-0-89486-221-2

Cover and interior design by David Spohn
Typesetting by Tursso Companies

INTRODUCTION

These do's and don'ts are ideas to use when you're trying to cope with problem drinkers or other drug abusers. I've gathered information from a number of mentors, particularly from the late Murray Bowen at the Georgetown Family Center. But the most important influence on my thinking came from the clients I've talked to over the years. These former clients are experts on the subject of addiction and the family; they're the experts who have graduated from the school of hard knocks. And, of course, some of these ideas I've picked up through my experience in my own family.

These ideas are one part of what this pamphlet is all about—how to turn those hard knocks into your own wisdom and help yourself. I hope these ideas will inspire you, but ideas are cheap, no matter how good they are. If you're trying to deal with the addiction of someone who's important to you, and if you're really in a jam, it isn't enough just to read about some good ideas. So there's another part to this pamphlet: a personal workbook. In a real sense, you too are going to be an author of this pamphlet.

It's important to quit suffering silently and get some work done to improve your life. Shifting into an active role is more easily said than done, however, so I want you to approach this pamphlet not just as something to read but also as a project.

Once you get started you'll find new courage, I think, to look at your situation clearly and honestly. I hope the exercises will inspire you to seek more information about addiction and calmly assess what needs to be done about your own situation—if anything at all. Finally, you should put together some careful plans for doing what you can to improve things.

The exercises require you to do some thinking, some research, and then some writing. Thoughtful work will make you feel stronger for action—when the time comes. After completing the workbook, you will realize that you have some answers and a better idea of where to find the rest of the answers. Your work on this project should make you feel that you really can take charge of your life in some ways—by taking simple steps, just one day at a time.

The truth is that when you're worn out from coping with addiction, no one else can pull you back in through the looking glass. Others can encourage you and give you good suggestions. But when all is said and done, you're going to have to make some decisions for yourself. And you can, if only you will. It's important that you participate in your own recovery program. One way to begin that is through working the exercises.

WHAT'S NORMAL?

When we're afraid that someone we care about is drinking too much, what do we do? When we suspect someone in our family is abusing drugs, what do we do? Most of us become pretty thoroughly wrapped up in the life of the addicted person. It's hard to give much thought to how we ourselves are involved in the problem.

We can't do anything to make the addict stop drinking or quit using. So usually we find ourselves blaming this sorry person for resisting all our helpful overtures. At the same time we probably kick ourselves for being so hopelessly ineffective.

It's normal for people to try to be reasonable—and logical. It's human nature to attempt to reason with people we care about once we know that things are going badly for them. But if we've been involved with an addicted person for any length of time, we know that trying to reason with a practicing addict can be discouraging. Addicts can teach us some mind-bending lessons in the art of debate. We may start out thinking that we're being reasonable but end up feeling as if we're losing our minds. Our best arguments tend to get us nowhere.

When reason fails, some of us resort to pleading with the addicted person. We may think our pleas are effective when we see them inspire regret and remorse. Only afterward do we realize that a guilty addict almost automatically becomes a drunk or stoned one. When we reinforce the self-hatred the addict feels, we give that person another good excuse to drink or use drugs again.

Eventually, we may try to lay down the law. We make heavy-duty threats of dire consequences if the drinking and drug use don't stop. Usually, this action isn't taken until we are desperate. The trouble is that if we're still overly involved with the addict by this time, we are also thoroughly hooked—into the addicted person.

When we care deeply about someone, it's easy to be caught up in a pattern of attempts to help, followed by failures, followed by still more desperate attempts. When things reach this state, there's little chance that we mean to give up. Addicts, who are often blessed with greater than average intuition, usually know us better than we know ourselves. They know what they can get away with and how far we can be pushed. When the time comes that we're making threats, they know we're just as determined to keep the game going as they are. But of course no one is conscious of any of this.

RIGID PATTERNS

Long after all of our efforts have failed, and long after good sense would tell us to give up, we usually try all of these strategies over again—the reasoning, the pleading, and the threatening. Dan Anderson, former president of Hazelden, refers to addiction as a "rigid stereotyped pattern of maladaptive behavior." These same words also describe the dedicated people who are caught up in someone else's addiction.

Eventually, we learn how to put up with the problems and live *around* them, one way or another. We develop strategies for anticipating trouble. We learn to endure more trouble than we could ever have imagined. And we discover how to pick up the pieces afterward so that the outside world will never know what's really happening.

We manage to avoid facing our situation again and again. The slightest ray of hope can distract us from the reality of our situation. The addict's promises are repeatedly broken, and our depression becomes another distraction from reality. And yet with incurable optimism, we're capable of looking straight ahead, pretending that everything will work itself out.

To sum it up, these are some of the ways in which normal people try to cope with alcoholism and drug abuse—doing the normal things that anyone would do. But it fails to get the job done—over and over again.

Naturally, anyone in this situation would like to be presented with a good solution. I don't want to deceive you with the appealing simplicity of the title of this workbook, *Do's and Don'ts for Family Members*. There may be some answers for you here, and I can tell you about some mistakes to avoid. But getting through this pamphlet is going to take some serious thought. You'll need to devote yourself to this project and show some genuine courage and dedication. You can improve your lot by changing your ways of dealing with someone else's addiction. I want you to find some creative new solutions. You can do it.

LETTING GO WITH LOVE

"Letting go" means doing whatever it takes to lower the level of anxiety that binds us to another person. Letting go is the surest, safest, and best thing that we can do for ourselves and for the troubled people we're trying to help. It's also the most difficult thing to do. We can always dream up a new angle or a new strategy for doing something about our own alcoholic or addict. It always seems easiest to keep on doing more of what we've been doing, no matter how many times we have endured painful experiences while trying to run the show ourselves.

It usually takes a heavy new jolt of thoughtfulness, humility, and courage for us to change our ways—to let go with love. But you won't understand much about what "letting go" means just from reading about it here. It's a concept that must be lived to be understood—and that living must happen a day at a time. It's a concept to be pondered. All I can do is provide you with some guidelines that help me when I try to practice what I'm preaching here. When you "get it," you'll come up with a definition that's all your own.

Among the many things that keep us wrapped up in someone else's problems is our fear—our apprehension. We're usually so worried about what will happen next that we don't see how we are keeping the pot boiling in spite of ourselves. We can't see how our own behavior provides phony reasons for the troubled person's behavior, how our eagerness to save the day or to cover up the problem helps it to go on.

We may think "letting go" means abandoning our loved one. Of course, it doesn't mean abandonment. Well, then, what does it mean? It means, for one thing, caring about someone without taking care of him or her quite so much. It means loving someone without being a watchdog. It means giving others the freedom to make their own mistakes. Letting go really means reconciling ourselves to *our* lives.

Still another roadblock may be our fear that we are being selfish. Many of us have made careers of taking care of the chemically dependent people in our lives while failing to give much thought to our own needs. Though we may have been a help and a comfort to them in some ways, our constant worrying about them took time away from the feeding of our own spirit. It may also have created a heavy burden for them. Taking better care of ourselves makes it easier for us to live with ourselves and for others to live with us. Far from being a selfish act, letting go with love can mark the first step toward genuinely loving and respectful relationships with others.

There are answers. There are things to do, and there are things to avoid. But to learn how it all works and then to make the right moves is not an easy matter. You'll have to roll up your sleeves and pitch into this task if you're going to cope effectively with chemical dependency in your family.

> Now begin reading these do's and don'ts—but remember that you must write in this pamphlet as well as read it! I can't tell you what to do. I can help you ask yourself the necessary questions. And I do encourage you to begin finding your own answers. These written exercises may help you get started on this very important work.

TAKE TIME OUT FOR REFLECTION.

Sometimes it's hard to imagine that anything can change for the better. So one first move for you to make is this one: quit running so hard! Take time out to reflect on what is happening in your life. If you can manage it, do this for a few minutes each day for a few days—a short time in the afternoon, part of an evening. Take a weekend if you can manage to get away that long. Somehow, give yourself enough time and space for some quiet reflection.

This is not self-indulgence; it's important for your own health. If you're going to come out even in your effort to help an addict, you need to have a clear head. You need to keep your wits about you. You need to be able to *think* instead of reacting emotionally to every crisis. There is hope, but you've got to slow yourself down enough to realize this.

Reflective time will help you sort things out so that you don't see everything in your life as uniformly awful. As you reflect, ask yourself the questions below and write your answers down.

What is good and joyful and meaningful about your life as it is right now?

What are the things about your life that you can no longer tolerate?

What is happening in your life that you may not like much but that you can get along with for the time being?

> Don't let coping with addiction become a full-time occupation. Life is too short for that. You can get off the merry-go-round. Stop now and size things up. Thoughtfully and carefully decide what needs to be done. Begin to do it.

YOU HAVEN'T CAUSED ANYONE TO DRINK TOO MUCH OR ABUSE DRUGS.

Here you are, caught up in someone's addiction problems. Possibly others in the family are blaming you for all the trouble. You may have felt that you were different somehow and that you could never find yourself in a spot like this. But you've had to think again about that. Now that reality is sinking in, there's something else that you must know. *You cannot make someone else get drunk or stoned.* Whatever made you think you could?

This whole thing is a mystery, something that we need to ponder in our hearts. When we care about others deeply, we tend to exaggerate our own roles in whatever happens to them. We believe that we have caused their problems, perhaps because if we acknowledge that they are just working out their own fates, we may feel we are less important in their lives. The fact that we are not responsible for the addiction is hard for many of us to understand.

How have you blamed yourself?

Don't punish yourself any longer for something that isn't your fault.

YOU HAVE BEEN DOING THE BEST YOU COULD TO BE HELPFUL.

Sure, you've made mistakes. But you have tried to help with everything you've got. And you're still trying.

Probably the biggest mistake you made was to believe that you could make someone stop drinking too much or stop using drugs. But the energy that you have put into that effort is now going to be turned toward getting your own act together, right?

To begin changing yourself, not someone else, is the only sure way. You didn't know that before, but now you do. Be kind to yourself, first of all. You need to forgive yourself for your misguided efforts to be helpful in the past.

If you can forgive yourself for failing to help the addict, you will be able to think more clearly about how to deal with the situation in the future.

Misguided attempts to be helpful (list the mistakes you made because you didn't know better):

> Shed all feelings of guilt about the past.

FIND OTHERS TO "TALK TURKEY" WITH ABOUT YOUR SITUATION.

Do you try to solve problems alone instead of letting people know what's happening and how you feel? If you do, now is a time to reach out to others—whether they're relatives, friends, or professional helpers.

Or maybe you're a talker who depends too much on others—giving others too much responsibility for your burdens. If so, you may need to reassess your situation—and your own responsibilities.

Others can be helpful to you. And it isn't necessary to embarrass yourself by baring your heart to them. It may turn out that no one can offer you any direct advice or help, but you will find that there are others who will understand how you feel. There's something very comforting in that. Talking to others can also be a reality check.

When you seek out others to talk to about your predicament, follow these three guidelines:

1. Don't look for sympathy. Remember the old saying "Sympathy kills." Look for people who will understand but who will also encourage you to help yourself.
2. Don't look for someone who can analyze your situation. That isn't going to help you either. You have probably spent too much time analyzing things already. Trying to figure out why someone is an addict can be very frustrating and usually doesn't lead anywhere anyway.
3. Be careful about advice that people offer. (And I include any advice that's offered in this pamphlet.) You are responsible for your own solution to the problem.

When you do talk with others, try to keep the conversation on the subject of *your* personal needs, *your* hopes and aspirations, rather than those of the addict. Talk to others about yourself and how you're doing. You're the only one who's reaching out for help. You're the one who can change.

Use the following space to write down a few of the needs you have right now, and some of your hopes for the future.

Needs:

Hopes:

> Don't try to handle everything by yourself, and don't look for others to do your work for you.
>
> Don't suffer silently. Give up trying to control the show, but don't give up.

TRY TO DISCOVER THE PATTERNS OF INTERACTION. DEFINE WHAT PART YOU PLAY IN THIS FAMILY INTERACTION. TRY NOT TO ASK "WHY?"

WHEN do episodes of drinking and drug abuse occur?

HOW are you involved in the beginning, the middle, and the end of these episodes?

WHO else is typically involved?

WHERE do these episodes take place?

HOW LONG do they last? HOW do they end?

WHAT are the consequences?

WHAT are the patterns in these episodes of drinking or drug abuse?

HOW are you involved in these patterns?

When you summon the courage to look hard at the patterns of family interaction around the episodes of drinking and drug abuse, your eyes will open to new ways of coping with your problems.

> Don't be afraid to face the facts.

DO BEGIN TO DISCOVER YOUR INNER STRENGTH.

In the past you have been alert to every action and word of the person you worry about. You could tell by the way the door closed what kind of mood the addict would be in. And after a certain amount of trouble, you began to be on edge much of the time, looking for more.

Too often daily life may have been a series of anxious testings and repeated disappointments. You frequently left your state of mind in the hands of someone you couldn't count on.

Now you must try to move through your days doing your own work, taking your rest, enjoying your play, living according to your own values and standards. You can use your own judgment and live according to your own timetable. The goal is not to get so upset so often or so easily.

Some creative actions you can take to change the daily pattern of your life include the following:

In the morning:
For example: Instead of quarreling through breakfast with your husband, who is nursing a hangover and reading the paper, put together a new breakfast routine that meets your own needs and follow through with it.

In the afternoon:
For example: Maybe you habitually worry all day about whether or

not the person you care about is at work, school, or wherever else he or she is supposed to be. Quit making phone calls to check up. Make late afternoon plans for yourself to do your own work or to be with people you can count on.

In the evening:
For example: Plan your evening meal, your work or social life, and your bedtime according to your own needs. Include the other person if you like. But be certain that you are true to your own plan. If you have to eat alone, that's okay for now. Don't miss an important event while waiting for the addict to show up. Go by yourself or with someone else. And don't let the addict distract you from other responsibilities you may have. Finally, don't ever stay up pacing the floor. Go to bed when you're tired.

> Avoid repeating your old mistakes over and over. Don't allow the old patterns to reestablish themselves.

WORK OUT A PLAN TO CHANGE HOW YOU REACT TO EACH CRISIS. MAKE A REALISTIC PLAN, A PLAN THAT YOU CAN CARRY THROUGH.

Now that you have learned something about the behavior patterns you're caught up in, you can see how to change your reactions to crises. Consider the following examples:

Maybe you have always paced the floor and worried while waiting up for your wife to come home, only to give her a lecture when she returned.

Next time, turn out the lights and go to bed at a reasonable hour. You might leave the front porch light on. If you really can't sleep because of your anxiety, fake it.

For years you have made excuses for your friend. You've bailed him out of jail. You have covered his bad checks. You've lent him money. And you've taken him to treatment centers.

The next time, can you let him spend the weekend in jail? You might go to see him during visiting hours and take him a book to read. But don't bail him out right away.

You've planned family get-togethers around his moods. You saw that the children didn't disturb him when he was high on drugs and alcohol. You tried to buy his happiness, even though you knew you couldn't. He came to depend on you so much that he hated you. Can you see how this situation happened? And can you see how destructive it was? How can someone break out of a rigid pattern like this?

One thing that might prompt some change would be for you to begin inviting someone close, a relative or friend, over to dinner once a week—no matter what shape your husband is in.

Don't wait for the addict to change. You can lead the way by making changes of your own. (But don't try to solve everything all at once.)

DO THINGS THAT MAKE YOU FEEL BETTER ABOUT YOURSELF.

When we let ourselves slip into patterns of reaction to an addict, we let ourselves down—mentally, physically, emotionally, and spiritually. We can begin to feel weary, run down, and worn out from the struggle. We find ourselves being more sensitive than usual, more critical of ourselves and others. In short, it's easy to become tired-out pains in the neck ourselves after we've been coping with addiction for a while.

And it's easy to blame the addict when you're no longer a big hit among your friends, when no one enjoys spending time with you. So what are you going to do about it? Decide to quit blaming others if your self-esteem is sliding downhill, and put together a plan to pick yourself up again.

A plan to improve mental health:
Examples: Things like planning and organization, rest and relaxation, avoiding hassles with others, strategies for stress reduction.

A plan to improve physical health:
Examples: Proper diet and exercise, quitting smoking, and physical checkups.

A plan to improve self-image:
Examples: Cultivate outside interests that you've thought about but never acted on, such as taking a sculpture class, joining an environmental group, beginning a new sport, making a new friend of someone you find interesting.

A plan to improve spiritual life:
Examples: Whatever feeds your spirit. Become active with a church or community group or explore the outdoors in a new way.

Don't let yourself down.

COLLECT SOME GOOD, OBJECTIVE INFORMATION ABOUT CHEMICAL DEPENDENCY AND FAMILY LIFE. GO TO THE EXPERTS.

Visit the library and ask for literature on this subject. Check the psychology section or the addictions section in your local bookstore for titles. Do some reading on the Web about addiction and families. Consult mental health professionals in your community. Talk to people at your local family counseling services and local public and private service agencies that can be sources of help. Ask questions of others at Al-Anon meetings or in other self-help group meetings. Compare notes with other people.

Who knows? You may be exaggerating your situation, and possibly chemical dependency is not really the problem in your family that you think it is. It's important not to remain in the dark about a matter like this. It is equally important that you not ignore signs and symptoms, that you face up to the fact of chemical dependency (if that is indeed the problem).

Available sources of information (location and phone numbers):

Alcoholism and addiction hotline numbers in your community:

Hospitals with detox and treatment programs:

Readers' services at libraries:

Physicians, psychologists, counselors, and other professionals:

Local councils on alcoholism:

Reliable Web sites:

> Don't worry needlessly because you lack information. There's plenty of good information available.

MAKE AN EMERGENCY PLAN.

At a time when you can think rationally about your problems, allow yourself to speculate about the worst possible scenario, the worst thing that could happen. Try to have a friend or two with you when you go through this. What would you do if the sky really did fall in?

An emergency plan includes a list of friends, neighbors, relatives, and professional helpers you can call for help if and when you need it.

- Do you have all the phone numbers you need?
- At what times are these people available to help you?
- When can you *not* reach them?
- Have you checked out all the hospitals that offer crisis services, as well as the emergency health and social service agencies?
- Do you have all the phone numbers and addresses for these places?
- Have you checked out legal services that might be available to you in an emergency?

This sort of rational preparation is not a way of looking for trouble. Instead, it's a way to keep you from worrying too much. If things go wrong, you will know what you need to do and what you can do.

Whom to call in the event of an emergency (names, phone numbers, addresses, notes about services available):

Don't sit on edge, frightened and waiting for the other shoe to fall. (It doesn't help to dwell on your emergency plan either.)

GO TO AL-ANON
(OR TO ANOTHER MUTUAL-HELP GROUP), WHERE PEOPLE WILL UNDERSTAND WHAT YOU'RE GOING THROUGH.

Al-Anon and other mutual-help groups can be part of your plan for rebuilding your life. Certainly in Al-Anon, but in other Twelve Step support groups as well, there are people who know what you're experiencing and who can encourage you with their own stories. They create an atmosphere where you can begin to sort things out for yourself.

People in Twelve Step groups won't give you specific advice about what to do with your life. Instead, they will be present for you and will hear you out with a good measure of understanding. They will tell you about their own stories. They will share their own experiences, strengths, and hopes with you. They will help you realize that you really aren't crazy, after all—that it just seems that way sometimes.

Mutual-help group resources:

Contact persons:

Meeting dates:

Meeting places:

Meeting times:

> Don't let your fears and mistrust keep you away from the bene-
> fits of mutual-help groups.

DO LEARN TO BE COMPASSIONATE
AS YOU PRACTICE LETTING GO.

In time, you'll learn to be a little more objective about addiction. You'll realize that you have not caused anyone's addiction and that you cannot cure it. You will begin taking better responsibility for your own life, and you will see this responsibility as something separate from your concern about someone else's addiction. You will begin to know that addiction is a devastating illness—that addicts are just people who struggle day after day with this illness.

When we're able to move back from our personal reactions, it becomes possible to see addicts as people again. Forget about all that's gone wrong. These are people we're talking about. When we realize this, any help that we offer becomes much more effective. The emotional benefits to our being able to feel compassion for the addict in our life will be very important to us. That's a promise.

List the good qualities the person you're concerned about has:

> Don't continue to be angry and resentful or suspicious and apprehensive.

LEARN TO LIVE ONE DAY AT A TIME.

This may be the key to the whole business of rebuilding. It means forgiving yourself and others for the past. And it means being hopeful but realistic about the future. It means living each day as fully as you can—enjoying your blessings and coping with the problems that each day may bring.

Living one day at a time is easier with the help of the Serenity Prayer:

God grant me the serenity
To accept the things I cannot change,
The courage to change the things I can,
And the wisdom to know the difference.

What one past hurt can you forgive right now?

What one worry can you give up today?

What particular blessing are you grateful for today?

> Don't give up hope. You can handle today!

Hazelden Classics for Families

In the past and present century alike, Hazelden has published the best known, most widely read literature that family members of alcoholics and addicts turn to for help and direction. Practical and compassionate, Hazelden's "classic" pamphlets provide solutions that have worked for generations of families as they heal and lead fulfilling lives.

Turning Hard Knocks into Wisdom

When you're worn out from coping with someone's addiction . . .
- do things that make you feel better about yourself
- do remember that you haven't caused anyone to drink too much

But remember . . .
- don't try to handle everything yourself
- don't wait for the addict to change

Part guidebook, part interactive workbook, *Do's and Don'ts for Family Members* presents time-proven ideas and thought-provoking questions to help family members deal with problem drinkers and other drug abusers, and move ahead to create their own recovery plan.

Pamphlets in the Hazelden Classics for Families series

Codependency
Detaching with Love
Do's and Don'ts for Family Members
Free to Care
A Guide for the Family of the Alcoholic

HAZELDEN®

15251 Pleasant Valley Road
P.O. Box 176
Center City, MN 55012-0176

1-800-328-9000 (Toll Free U.S. and Canada)
1-651-213-4000 (Outside the U.S. and Canada)
1-651-213-4590 (Fax)

www.hazelden.org

Order No. 1235

ISBN 978-0-89486-221-2

90000

9 780894 862212